# Tabletops

# Tabletops

Jo Rigg

Over 30 projects for inspirational table decorations

BULFINCH PRESS

AOL Time Warner Book Group

BOSTON • NEW YORK • LONDON

First United States Edition

ISBN 0-8212-2881-8
Library of Congress Control Number 2002108547

Bulfinch Press is a division of AOL Time Warner Book Group.

Printed in Hong Kong

# contents

# introduction

Tabletops is packed with imaginative table settings, quick styling ideas, and hints and tips for creating the perfect look, whatever your taste and whatever the occasion. Whether you are planning a family get-together or a sophisticated holiday dinner, *Tabletops* shows you how to pull together all the right elements to create the perfect atmosphere and make any event memorable. The emphasis is on fun, and on combining color and a few well-chosen accessories to conjure up a host of exciting new looks for tables in both indoor and outdoor settings.

Alongside the deceptively simple ideas for creating themed table settings such as a french bistro or a tropical party, you will find step-by-step projects for decorated napkins and tablecloths, painted glasses, stamped bowls, punched tin lanterns, and gorgeous floral centerpieces. All the techniques used are inexpensive, quick, and deliver foolproof results. So take pleasure in making your table look inviting. Choose a theme, set the scene, and make every meal an occasion to remember!

Blue and white is a truly classic combination—clean and fresh yet calm and soothing. A bold checkered tablecloth and utility striped napkins form the basis of this table design, and the overall look is brought up to date with modern cutlery and chunky juice glasses. Keeping to a rigid color scheme such as this one allows all kinds of patterns and styles to be combined successfully. For a timeless but contemporary feel, mix together different shades of blue—soft powder blue, intense cobalt, inky indigo—with pure white.

# blue and white

Breakfast is the most important meal of the day, so why not make an extra-special effort to enjoy it? Here the blue-and-white tablecloth provides the perfect backdrop for the warm tones of the breakfast food, making it look even more appetizing: golden croissants that melt in your mouth, soft yellow butter, zesty grapefruit, and delicious apricot preserves look mouthwateringly good. A jug of spring flowers adds height to the table design and provides a natural element that complements the geometric and striped patterns used in this scheme.

A plain china teapot and country-style tea set continue the traditional feel of this charming breakfast table. Choose different designs to suit your personal style: polka dots and floral prints, and large- and small-scale patterns can be used successfully as long as you keep to the basic color scheme. Enhance the rustic mood by making fabric tops to cover store-bought preserves. Cut a circle of fabric a little wider than the diameter of the lid and tie it to the top of the jar with a pretty blue-and-white ribbon. The scent of grape hyacinths, marguerites, and forget-me-nots gathered straight from the garden is the perfect finishing touch for this inviting breakfast table. So pull back the curtains and let the morning sunlight flood in!

A tangy yogurt and a handful of blueberries are the perfect healthy way to begin your day.

Chunky blue glasses add a contemporary feel to the table.

**MATERIALS**
tea towel
pins
tape measure
needle and thread
ribbon

A cutlery roll cleverly made from a cotton tea towel keeps cutlery together and looks so pretty it can be left out on the table. Blue-handled cutlery completes the blue-and-white theme!

**1** Lay the tea towel face down and fold about a third of it over on itself to form an envelope. Secure it with pins.

# cutlery roll

**2** Using the tape measure, mark out channels in the folded tea towel with the pins.

**3** Stitch the two layers of the tea towel together along the pinned channels, removing the pins as you sew.

**4** Fill the channels with cutlery and roll up tightly.

**5** Wrap a length of ribbon around the cutlery roll and tie it in a bow.

The next time you plan to spend an evening at home enjoying an Asian meal, transform it into a stylish event with a few simple touches. This table has been given a modern Asian feel that is clean and minimalist yet delicate and feminine. Traditional Chinese elements have been reinterpreted in Western style to create a look of balanced sophistication. The lilac silk tablecloth is embroidered with a trellis design, which counterbalances the clean lines of the plain bowls and plates to give an overall impression of delicate, simple beauty.

# asian style

Another pretty touch is introduced by the lilac orchid stem, the shape of its petals emphasized by the roundness of the pale pink vase. Spherical and circular shapes are used across the table, from the cylindrical water glasses to the round teapot and globular paper lanterns, and soft pastel shades tie the scheme together, creating a harmonious look that is easy on the eye. The dark pink centers of the orchids and the red detail in our woven chopstick runner ensure that the table does not look bland, yet these bright colors are present in such small splashes that they don't unsettle the calm sophistication of the overall design.

Asian supermarkets are a great of source of food-and-drinks packaging that has decorative pictures or lettering that is pretty enough to be left out on display rather than hidden away in a kitchen cupboard. Serving jasmine tea from a Chinese-style teapot is another nice touch, especially if the tea is drunk from small bowls rather than cups and saucers. Find bowls and plates with interesting glazes, and use brightly colored chopsticks for a contemporary fusion style. Inexpensive Chinese paper lanterns also have instant impact when laid across a table or used to bring a soft light to the room. Fortune cookies and Asian medallions add to the sense of occasion. Eat up and enjoy!

A single orchid stem looks stunning placed in a modern glass vase.

An Asian medallion and some ribbon transform a plain napkin, and fortune cookies add an element of fun to the meal.

MATERIALS
2 skeins red
  embroidery thread
scissors
100 bamboo
  chopsticks

A table runner made from wooden chopsticks woven together is elegant yet practical, protecting the pale and delicate silk tablecloth from hot dishes and accidental spillages. The red embossed Chinese lettering adds a pretty touch.

# chopstick runner

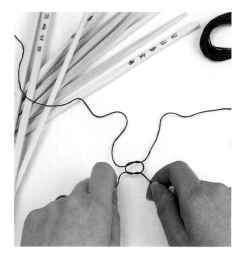

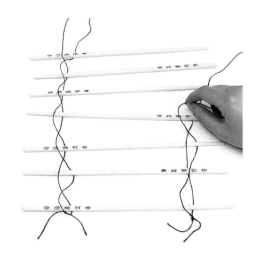

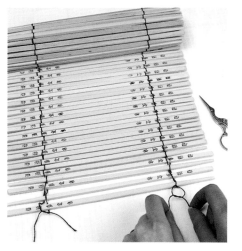

**1** Take four 40-inch lengths of red embroidery thread. Tie two lengths together. Tie the remaining two lengths together so that you now have two double-up lengths of thread.

**2** Lay both pairs of thread on the table with the knotted ends closest to you. Place the chopsticks on the table, making sure that the writing is visible, and weave the threads alternately under and over each chopstick, pushing them together.

**3** Once all of the chopsticks have been used, tie the threads to keep the chopsticks in place. Trim off the ends of the threads for a neat finish.

Spring is a magical time of year, the signs of new life welcome after a long winter. Mark the return of blue skies with a gathering of friends and family over a simple meal. Keep the table decoration light and fresh to match the mood, and bring elements of the new season into your home to create a celebratory atmosphere. An elegant stemmed glass makes a pretty holder for this simple Easter flower arrangement (*right*). Delicate grape hyacinths are surrounded by fluffy feathers in a powder-blue duck egg. A length of ribbon tied to the stem adds the finishing touch.

# easter pastel

Tiny egg-shape salt-and-pepper shakers look lovely on an Easter breakfast table with a soft-boiled egg and toast.

The delicate fragrance of these grape hyacinths is the very epitome of spring.

A windfall nest filled with different kinds of eggs completes this simple Easter table, setting the scene for a delicious breakfast. Yellow feathers and spring-flowering forsythia add delicate contrast to the blues on the table, bringing warm spring sunshine indoors.

MATERIALS
food coloring
small bowl of
    water
white marabou
    feathers
paper towels
plate

1 Add a few drops of food coloring to the bowl of water. Leave the feathers in the water for about five minutes so they can soak up the color.

# dyed marabou feathers

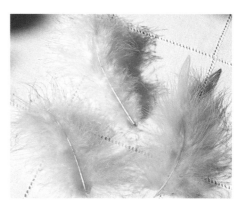

2 Lay the wet feathers on the paper towels to soak up any excess water. Allow to dry in a warm place for a few hours.

3 Once the feathers are dry, smooth them very gently with your fingertips until they soften and become fluffy.

4 To make different colored feathers simply repeat steps 1 to 3 using food coloring in other colors.

A quintessentially English afternoon tea is the perfect occasion to indulge in a riot of floral patterns and gilt edges. A centerpiece of garden roses and hydrangeas in shades of red and pink sets the scene perfectly. Serve treats—scones split in two then heaped with jam and extra-thick cream—and a variety of other tempting cakes and savory goodies. Cucumber sandwiches with the crusts cut off, fresh strawberries or petits fours are other traditional teatime treats that are guaranteed to delight your guests.

# afternoon tea

For such a refined affair, only the best table linen will do. Pure white linen napkins and a matching tablecloth are a must, as are dainty cake forks and teaspoons. You could mix lots of different patterns on your table for an eclectic look, or stick to one pattern for a more refined feel—the choice is yours! Classic floral designs all combine well, and adding some plain pieces will prevent the scheme from becoming too overwhelming. Chintz china evokes images of English summer gardens in bloom, and harks back to a time gone by when afternoon tea was a daily event. The term chintz comes from the Indian word *chintes* and is used to describe colorful patterns, including richly hued flowers and brightly plumed birds.

Unusual floral napkin decorations can be made by attaching fabric rosebuds to bands of fabric-covered elastic and are a lovely way to welcome guests to the table. In addition to napkins to catch the crumbs, guests are bound to need cake forks to attack those delicious crumbly cakes and sticky, jam-laden scones. A cake stand adds a real sense of occasion to the table and makes it easy for an array of goodies to be passed around. A good quality bone china teapot is a must, and this and the sugar bowl and milk jug can be as decorative as you wish. Remember to keep refilling the teapot so there is a plentiful supply of hot, fresh tea to accompany all those lovely cakes.

A gilt sugar bowl and matching milk jug look perfect with the gilt-edge china.

For a fun touch embellish sugar cubes with gel icing in colors to coordinate with your teacups.

Roses and hydrangeas are the only flowers needed to make this stunning wreath. We have chosen flowers in shades that match the china on the table so as to ensure a really colorful display. Made in an instant, this centerpiece can't fail to impress your guests.

**MATERIALS**
large round bowl
ring of wet oasis,
    10 inches in
    diameter
moss
florist's wire
secateurs or
    strong scissors
pink hydrangeas
red and pink
    roses

# floral centerpiece

1 Fill the bowl with water and soak the oasis until it is fully saturated. Remove the oasis from the bowl, shaking off any excess water.

2 Cover the oasis in moss, securing it with florist's wire.

3 Cut the hydrangea stems so that they are about 2 inches long. Add the flowers evenly around the ring.

4 Finish the arrangement by adding groups of three or four roses between the hydrangea heads until no moss is visible.

Bright, exotic colors combined with natural fabrics and lots of flowers set the scene for a tropical-inspired party. Don't worry about coordinating the colors: the more vibrant tones you can pack onto the table the better. Let your imagination run wild with fruit and flower displays, choosing only the most brilliant hues for a tropical riot of color. A lively theme such as this makes a wonderful setting for a summer barbeque or evening garden party. As night begins to fall, our recycled tin can lanterns illuminate the tropical table, creating a delightful atmosphere.

# tropical party

Dusky pink stargazer lilies add extra color to our tropical spread, but any brightly colored flowers could be used. Giant proteas or purple vanda orchids would look equally stunning. You might like to decorate the room with plastic or paper flowers too for a touch of kitsch! Tropical fruit such as pineapple, passion fruit, and papaya are now readily available year round, and form the centerpiece of this display. The simple burlap tablecloth is the perfect backdrop for the vibrant fruit and pink lilies and contrasts well with the green of the banana leaf.

Using banana leaves as a platter for the fruit is an exotic touch that looks perfect: you could be in the Caribbean! (Be sure to rinse them first.) Make a fabulous tropical fruit salad for your guests and serve it in melon baskets (*below*). Serve delicious cocktails made with the juice from some of your exotic fruit: try pineapple juice with a dash of lime topped with soda for a long refreshing drink, or blend a variety of fruits together to create your very own fruit punch. Add cocktail umbrellas and brightly colored swizzle sticks for a fun look. Floating small fruits or pieces of larger fruits in the cocktails is another lovely touch, and if you skewer them onto cocktail sticks first, guests will be able to nibble them easily.

A stargazer lily laid in a palmwood bowl is a lovely place setting for each guest.

When you have cut the flesh out of a melon why not reuse the sturdy skin as a serving bowl?

These wonderful silver lanterns are made from old tin cans—holes punched into the metal allow the glow of a tealight to shine through. Try using a variety of cans and punching different patterns into them to make an array of lanterns.

**MATERIALS**
permanent marker
tin can, washed
nail
hammer
tealight candle

**1** Using a permanent marker, draw your pattern on the can with dots.

# tin can lantern

**2** Place the nail over a dot and hammer it through the can. Remove the nail.

**3** Continue hammering the nail through the can until all of the dots have become holes.

**4** Place a tealight inside the lantern and light it using a long match or taper.

Memories of long summer days spent by the ocean during lazy weekends or family vacations are often some of our most precious. Be inspired by the muted tones and wave-smoothed edges of driftwood, pebbles, and shells to create a table that reawakens seaside memories. Treasures collected from the shore can be used to decorate a picnic table made from a sun-bleached board. Shell place cards make charming keepsakes, and pebbles make excellent weights to prevent napkins from flying away in the breeze—and they can be left on the beach when you leave!

# beach party

Paper napkins printed with a shell design are both decorative and practical. A pretty mother-of-pearl spoon with a shell handle is a fitting piece for a beach table.

A simple row of pebbles adorns this contemporary china plate; a pebble candle keeps the beach theme.

Placing salt and pepper in cleaned oyster shells is a lovely touch.

A folded square of plain card makes a perfect base for these elegant place cards. By altering the type and number of shells used, the cards can be made simpler or more elaborate. Their real beauty is that no two will be exactly the same.

**MATERIALS**
pencil
metal ruler
white card
scalpel or craft
  knife
non-water soluble
  liquid glue
shells

# shell place cards

**1** Using the pencil and ruler, draw a 4 inch square on the card. Cut it out with the scalpel and ruler.

**2** Draw a faint line across the middle of the card and lightly score along it with the scalpel. Fold the card along the score line.

**3** Lightly dip each of the shells in glue and position them on the card. Allow to dry overnight, then neatly write a name on each card.

Bistro-style dining is a wonderful way to enjoy an informal meal, a tasty snack or just a relaxing coffee and croissant. Imagine yourself sitting in a pretty Parisian side street sipping a refreshing citron pressé and watching the world go by, or chatting with friends over an evening glass of wine by the seafront in Deauville. Here (*right*) we have created an arrangement with bistro-style dining in mind. The round chrome table captures the chic elegance of a city bistro, and the use of bold red and white napkins and tablecloth gives a truly French feel.

# french bistro

The table looks busy and interesting, yet great care has been taken not to overdress it. Every item on the table—from the salt and pepper pots to the water carafe—has been carefully chosen to emphasise the bistro style. Our sponged bowls are the perfect size for soup, moules marinières or salad, and the technique is so simple that you can quickly create enough bowls for the whole family. Make sure you provide plenty of French bread and some delicious herb-marinated olives to nibble on while you chat. Simple glassware is as versatile as the bowls and can be used for water, fruit juice, or robust red wine, depending on your preference.

Apart from the single red gerbera placed in one of the larger chunky glasses, everything on our table has a practical use, so the setting avoids looking fussy or overdone. Napkins were chosen to match the square of red and white cloth that covers the center of the table, contrasting with the cool color of the chrome and bringing a lively, vibrant feel to the arrangement. A wine bottle holds a candle, ready to be lit as evening falls. Tie a square of gingham fabric around the bottle for some instant Gallic chic. Oil and vinegar bottles held in a neat chrome rack sit alongside a classic glass cruet set, and robust glasses complete the practical feel of the table.

This simple white bowl is large enough to hold plenty of slices of freshly baked baguette.

Dip chunks of bread into olive oil and balsamic vinegar, or spread them with creamy unsalted butter.

**MATERIALS**
red ceramic paint
small plate
small square
 sponge
medium-size
 paintbrush
plain ceramic bowl

Versatile and robust tableware is perfect for bistro-style eating. Chunky white bowls sponged with red ceramic paint make a striking addition to the table and are very easy to make.

# sponged bowl

**1** Pour some ceramic paint onto the plate. Dip the sponge in the paint and lightly sponge the outside of the bowl. Set aside until the paint is dry.

**2** With the paintbrush, paint a fine line around the base of the bowl. Allow to dry.

**3** Paint another fine line around the rim of the bowl. Allow to dry, then bake in the oven following the paint manufacturer's instructions.

Life on the water and all things nautical are the inspiration for this table design. An ocean map used as a table covering sets the seafaring scene, and carefully chosen sea-inspired accents complete the nautical theme. Introducing miniature boats is a fun way to decorate a nautical table, and children and adults alike will love to play with them while they relax over a leisurely lunch. Sisal rope place mats the color of sandy beaches are robust and durable, and look delightful next to the soft blues and turquoises of the other elements on the table.

# nautical lunch

A navy blue storm lantern will cast a lovely flickering light over the table as dusk approaches, creating a magical atmosphere. Subtly tinted blue wine glasses and tumblers were chosen for this setting, their slightly bubbly texture reminiscent of rippling waves glistening in the sun. The cutlery has transparent blue handles, which evoke the color of the ocean. Continue the nautical theme by serving guests a seafood platter on a bed of ice and seaweed, or whole freshly grilled fish. As for aperitifs, what could be more refreshing than a sea breeze cocktail? Decorating desserts with fish-shape candies will delight your guests, and shell-shape chocolates make a delicious accompaniment to coffee!

Whether you are eating at the ocean or recreating the nautical mood at home, hang colorful bunting alongside your table. Made from assorted triangles of red and blue patterned fabrics, it will cheer up even the dullest day. Search through toy boxes for little boats and flags, and hunt along the tideline for interesting shells, pebbles, sea-smoothed glass, and driftwood: lots of fun can be had collecting nautical-theme accessories. Asking guests to bring along their own nautical items is a great conversation starter. If you choose fairly heavy objects they can double as paperweights to hold down the map tablecloth if the sea breeze becomes a gusty wind.

The simple swirl of blue on the plates repeats the spiral of the rope place mats underneath.

Name cards or messages placed inside a small bottle with a little sand and stopped with a cork are bound to charm guests.

A length of rope is wound around itself in a spiral to make this sturdy place mat. As rope is so durable, even the hottest plate won't damage the mat or the table under it. The color looks great too set against the soft blues on the table.

**MATERIALS**
½ inch diameter
  sisal rope
non-water soluble
  liquid glue
pins
pliers

# rope place mat

**1** Roughly curl the rope into a loose spiral and run a row of small glue spots along the first 12 inches of the spiral.

**2** Curl the rope into a tight spiral, inserting pins at intervals to hold the coils in place.

**3** To finish the spiral add a little extra glue to the end of the rope length and pin it in place. Allow to dry overnight then remove any pins that are showing with pliers.

Whatever the occasion may be—perhaps simply that the sun is shining—why not organize a summer garden party? Pretty, soft pastel colors are the order of the day in this scheme because they look wonderful in the sunlight. Our table contains nothing that has been slavishly sought after or that takes a long time to put together—even the organza tablecloth can be made in less than half a day. The spirit of this table setting is simplicity and ease. With a little ingenuity and a few quick creative touches you can achieve fabulous results with minimal effort.

# summer party

Paper lanterns hung from branches—or from a large garden parasol—cost just a few cents each, but look fantastic as they stir in the breeze. Pretty bottle stoppers add another decorative touch and also prevent tiny leaves, blossoms, or curious insects from dropping into the wine! Set out an array of salads and cold food so guests can help themselves, rather than serving a more formal lunch where food arrives at the table already arranged on plates. On our table shiny steep-sided trays hold food that can be informally passed around at this casual summer party. They also make the transportation of items from the kitchen to the garden as easy as can be. So sit back, relax with your guests and enjoy the sunshine!

Paper lanterns create a sense of occasion, and the theme is continued in the sheets of handmade paper rolled into cones and packed with luscious summer fruits. Tied with lengths of ribbon, cones are the perfect shape for even young children to hold, and have the added advantage of not needing to be washed once lunch is over! A quick search around the garden can provide a variety of flowers for the table. Simply cut off some blooms and arrange them in an assortment of glass bottles or jars of various heights to create a delightful display. Blue tealight holders look great set against the pink and blue of the tablecloth.  Burning tealights scented with citronella also have the advantage of keeping mosquitos at bay.

A large jug of ice water flavored with sprigs of mint provides welcome refreshment on a hot day.

Bring out ice in these lovely colored ice trays: their interesting shapes are sure to be a conversation starter.

**MATERIALS**
scissors
12-inch length of
   blue sheer fabric,
   48 inches wide
tape measure
pink organza to
   cover your table
glitter fabric paint

Lovely effects can be created by layering sheer fabrics in different colors and bonding them with fabric paint. Here we have bonded blue rectangles of sheer fabric onto soft pink organza for a summery tablecloth.

# organza tablecloth

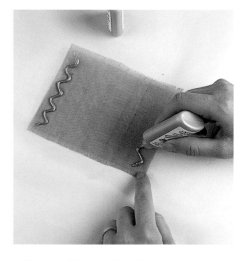

**1** Measure eight rectangles 5 x 7 inches on the blue fabric and cut them out.

**2** Carefully fray the edges of each rectangle and then position them on the pink organza.

**3** Zigzag glitter fabric paint onto each rectangle and stick it onto the organza cloth. Allow to dry overnight.

Rich spicy colors and gorgeous fabrics come to mind when thinking about ethnic style. The look is opulent and elaborate with a hot palette of deep reds, oranges, and vibrant pinks. For our ethnic table design, colors that may seem almost too bold at first sight are combined to good effect, and small touches of gold and silver enhance the opulent feel without making the table look gaudy. Find tableware that has strong colors and robust shapes to recreate the look. A deep red silk tablecloth stamped with a gold pattern is the basis for this ethnic table setting.

# ethnic ambience

The floral centerpiece continues the deep red color but gives the table a modern feel with roses and bamboo arranged in individual shot glasses in a square dish. The dark green foliage and brighter green bamboo shoots bring freshness to the overall table design. White plates with gold patterning lighten the table setting and prevent it from looking too dark. Indian samosas and onion bhajis are served on deep-gold dishes that look fabulous against the red tablecloth. Tea glasses in rich, jewel-like colors make wonderful holders for incense sticks, which will give the room a heady fragrance. Spicy scents mingle with the rich colors on the table to create a warm ambience.

Tealight holders in ruby red glass enhance the richness of this table design, and the deep colors of the rest of the table look lovely when illuminated by the flickering candlelight. Creating such an opulent table setting doesn't have to cost a lot: a few stitches of metallic embroidery thread liven up a plain napkin, and inexpensive Indian bangles make unusual yet stunningly simple napkin rings. Choose plates and cutlery that echo the ethnic style of the tablecloth and accessories—here, the swirly gold pattern on the plates picks up on the gold in the tablecloth and is echoed in the spiral detail at the ends of the knives and forks. Incense sticks add the final touch, their pungent aroma filling the room with Eastern flavor.

Three gold bangles are cleverly put to use as a napkin ring.

Regimented rows of deep red roses and fresh green bamboo on a bed of gold sand create a modern centerpiece.

Using wooden stamps to apply patterns to cloth is an ancient technique. Sophisticated patterns using many colors can be achieved by applying different stamps over the same area, but using one color alone can create an equally stunning effect.

**MATERIALS**
length of silk
pins
needle
thread to match
   the silk
scissors
gold fabric paint
wooden printing
   blocks
paintbrush

**1** Turn the raw edges of the fabric under and use pins to hold them in place. With the needle and thread stitch all the way around the fabric to give a neat edge.

# stamped tablecloth

**2** For the border, apply fabric paint to the wooden printing block with the paint brush. Remember you only need to cover the part that will touch the cloth.

**3** Firmly press the block down onto the edge of the silk and hold it for a few seconds. Apply another coat of paint and place the block next to the first print, pressing down firmly. Continue all around the edge of the cloth.

**4** For the flower design, take the second printing block and apply fabric paint as in step 2. Stamp at regular intervals across the central area of the cloth, remembering to apply a fresh coat of paint each time.

A sparkling glass of champagne is synonymous with celebration, evoking as it does feelings of triumph, success, and excitement. The sound of corks popping is a fabulous party icebreaker, and the bubbly cascade as the champagne is poured from the bottle makes a wonderful noise.  This makes champagne—and other sparkling drinks—ideal for special occasions such as weddings, graduations, and anniversaries. A white linen tablecloth freshly ironed and laid on the drinks table creates a classic, elegant look and allows the warm color of the wine to stand out.

# champagne celebration

Dainty, bite-size canapés are ideal at a champagne party, as they allow guests to hold a glass in one hand while selecting delicious nibbles with the other. If you can't get hold of true champagne—which comes from a small area of northeastern France only—many wine-producing areas of the world have their own sparkling wines, so you can be sure to find a delicious alternative. A nonalcoholic drink that children will enjoy is a bubbly glass of sparkling ginger ale. Champagne may be drunk from a variety of glasses, though tall, elegant flutes serve the purpose best. Our simple painted glass project shows how easy it is to personalize them with dots of gold paint.

For a summer party, float fruit in the bubbles—strawberries and blueberries work well—or serve pink champagne as a refreshing alternative. With their unique shape, champagne corks can be put to good use after popping as fun place card holders. Simply make a slit in the top of each cork with a sharp knife and insert the place cards. Dispense drinks from large silver platters to bring Hollywood-style glamour to the event, and don't forget to keep the champagne cold in an elegant ice bucket! Mixing champagne cocktails is great fun, and stylish swizzle sticks look great when left in the glass.

The traditional shallow glass may look glamorous, but it allows those wonderful bubbles to escape too quickly!

These mini champagne towers are a twist on the traditional multilayered tower, but still have great appeal.

MATERIALS
plain glass flutes
gold outliner glass
    paint

Whatever your reason for drinking champagne, these beautiful handpainted glasses will make it an extra-special occasion. Decorated with a design inspired by all those bubbles, the glasses will sparkle and shimmer in the light.

# painted glasses

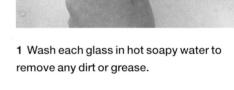

**1** Wash each glass in hot soapy water to remove any dirt or grease.

**2** Holding the glass by the stem, paint the bottom four "bubbles" using the gold outliner paint.

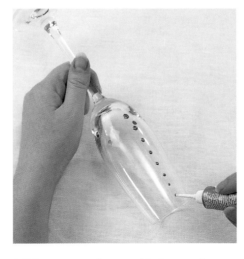

**3** When you are happy with the spacing, complete one line of bubbles. By applying a smaller amount of paint each time, the bubbles will decrease in size.

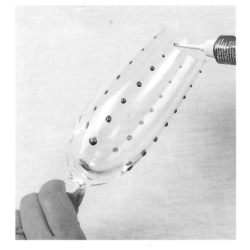

**4** Continue around the glass until each line of bubbles is complete. Allow to dry then bake in the oven following the paint manufacturer's instructions.

An invigorating walk in the woods is a chance to get back in tune with nature, so take a deep breath and let the fresh air clear your mind of the trials and tribulations of everyday life. Stop for a moment and take a good look around. Depending on the time of year you could find new green sprigs or glorious heaps of leaves in magnificent earthy browns, oranges, and rust colors. Build a table scheme around their vibrant colors, shapes, and textures. This table scheme is based around a display of fresh summer leaves and chunky church candles.

# woodland walk

Group a variety of leaves together in slender shot glasses to make a delicate and fresh display.

This clear glass tableware allows the beauty and texture of the natural twig mat to show through.

Arrange fern leaves beneath a clear glass plate. Their intricate leaf shape makes them ideal for a table display.

A group of decorated candles set on a table makes a stunning centerpiece, bringing some woodland serenity indoors. Leaves and bark are simply glued in place, and different effects can be created by varying the type of leaves used, or by layering them.

**MATERIALS**
natural leather
 twine
church candles
scissors
glue stick
selection of
 leaves and bark

# wrapped candles

**1** Measure a length of leather twine that is just over twice the circumference of the candle, then cut.

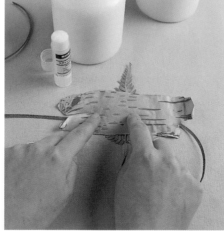

**2** Lay the twine face down and apply a small amount of glue along the length of it. Place the fern leaf face down on the twine and press it to secure.

**3** Place the bark on top of the fern leaf, again face down.

**4** Place the arrangement gently around the candle, tying the twine decoratively at the front.

When summer days carry with them a hint of autumn, the rewards of a season spent tending vegetable plots and gardens become apparent. Now is the time to harvest that glut of homegrown produce and hold an impromptu feast. But whether the salads and vegetables come straight from your garden or the local supermarket, eating outdoors on a summer's evening is always a delight.  If you don't have a large garden, divide up all the food and other necessities among your guests and head for the nearest park.

# garden gathered

Inspired by such a charming natural setting, dining can be a simple affair. Here (*right*) a makeshift table constructed from wooden planks set on a pair of trestles creates the ideal surface on which to lay an outdoor feast. Vegetable sacks sewn together with gardener's twine make the perfect rustic tablecloth, but make sure you wash the sacks thoroughly first to get rid of any dust that may be trapped in the fabric. (Sewing the sacks is a project that some younger members of the party might enjoy.)

Keep table arrangements casual, choosing colors and textures that complement that lazy late-summer mood. A large glazed jug packed with crisp corncobs and magnificent sunflowers looks glorious when matched with rustic tableware, brightly colored cutlery, and our easy-to-make harvest napkins. Handfuls of peppery nasturtium flowers and tiny leaves tossed into a green salad look stunning and taste fabulous. As a finishing touch, chalk the guests' names on old roof slates for unusual place settings or use one—as here—to display a selection of creamy French cheeses.

The combination of plenty of fresh air and lots of good food can make guests a little drowsy!

The photo-transfer method is simple to follow, making it easy to design harvest napkins for all the family.

Images of luscious vegetables transferred onto colorful napkins add interest and fit the setting perfectly. Good sources of suitable motifs are old gardening catalogs and seed packets. Use the napkins to carry bundles of cutlery to the table.

MATERIALS
black and white
  photocopies
scissors
image transfer paste
paintbrush
plain napkin
rolling pin
water
sponge

1 Take a photocopy of your chosen image and cut neatly around the edges with scissors.

# harvest napkins

2 Apply a thick layer of image transfer paste to the right side of the photocopy. The paste should completely cover the image.

3 Place the image paste-side down on a clean, ironed napkin and go over it with a rolling pin or your fingers. Allow to dry.

4 Lay a water-soaked sponge on top of the image. The top layer of copy paper can be peeled away once it is wet. Wipe away the remaining paper with the damp sponge.

5 When the napkin is dry, brush a final layer of image transfer paste over the image to seal it. Follow the paste manufacturer's instructions for washing the napkin.

Modern Halloween celebrations have their roots in ancient Celtic festivals, and the night traditionally marks the transition from autumn to winter. It is also the night on which the souls of the departed are supposed to revisit their homes to warm themselves by the fireside! It is no wonder, then, that stories of ghosts and ghouls abound at this time of year, and children love to dress up in suitably scary attire and go trick-or-treating around the neighborhood. Welcome them home with a cozy Halloween-themed supper of bowls of piping-hot soup with crusty bread.

# halloween

For an authentic Halloween atmosphere, decorate the table with rustic tableware in warm tones of orange and gold, and be sure to include an array of our jack-o'-lanterns. In days gone by, these were often displayed in front of the house, where they were thought to ward off evil spirits. A table decorated with a line of lanterns has a magical glow that instantly sets the scene for a Halloween celebration. All sorts of gourds can be used to create lanterns, or simply piled in a shallow bowl as another decoration; there are many types available and a variety of colors, shapes, and sizes look good when arranged together.

Another simple, decorative touch is to tie dried corncobs together and hang them on the front door to welcome guests. Serving hot soup out of a hollowed-out pumpkin is sure to delight your guests, and sprinkling fresh herbs and roasted pumpkin seeds on top of each bowlful will make it even more appetizing. The scooped-out insides of all types of squash can be used to make delicious soups or pies—or try roasting chunks in the oven. Dry pumpkin seeds in a warm oven and thread them together to create rustic napkin rings (*opposite, bottom left*). Candied apples are another delicious Halloween treat. Wrapping ribbons around their sticks adds a festive touch that both children and adults will appreciate.

Homemade soup served in chunky rustic tableware looks and tastes fantastic.

A large bowl of gourds in different shapes and colors makes an attractive table display.

Freshly baked bread cut at the table is the perfect accompaniment to hot soup.

pumpkin or squash
sharp knife
spoon
magic marker
tealight candle

Great fun can be had carving scary faces into hollowed-out pumpkins and squashes. Because a sharp knife is used in this project, let children draw the face on the pumpkin, but then make sure an adult does the carving in order to avoid accidents.

# jack-o'-lantern

**1** Using a sharp knife, cut the top off the pumpkin. This will form the lid. (Cut a slice off one side of the lid so smoke can escape.)

**2** Take the spoon and scoop out the seeds from inside the pumpkin. Then, using the knife, scrape out any excess. The walls of the pumpkin should be about an inch thick.

**3** Draw a scary face on the outside of the pumpkin with a magic marker.

**4** Carefully cut out the face with a sharp knife.

**5** Place a tealight inside the pumpkin and put the lid on. Light the candle with a long match through the mouth of the carved face.

The highlands of Scotland are the inspiration behind this simple table design. Set on a coarse linen cloth, natural elements are brought in to evoke a feeling of the dramatic, rugged nature of the Scottish mountains. Serve your guests a simple supper of Scottish smoked salmon and crusty whole-grain bread. A scattering of coarsely ground black pepper and a generous squeeze of fresh lemon juice are the perfect accompaniments. No highland supper could be complete without the incorporation of tartan: we chose a pretty ribbon to tie up a bundle of oatcakes.

# highland supper

For an eclectic look, mix together cutlery with different horn and bone handles.

A rolled linen napkin in a pewter ring with a sprig of heather will bring an instant highland spirit to your table.

The muted tones of our tartan ribbon work well with the natural colors featured on this table.

Candlelight has a magical quality and transforms a room instantly. This candle, made from natural beeswax, looks perfect surrounded by thistlelike sea holly and pheasant feathers. The delicate scent of honey will fill the room when the candle is lit.

# rolled candle

**MATERIALS**
3 sheets of natural beeswax, 8 inches wide
cotton wick, 10 inches long
scissors

**1** Place the first sheet of beeswax on a flat surface. Lay the wick along the shorter edge of the sheet.

**2** Fold the edge of the beeswax over on itself, around the wick, and begin rolling.

**3** Continue rolling the sheet as tightly as you can, keeping the edges straight.

**4** To add another sheet, lay the part-rolled candle on top of the new sheet. Carefully align the edges and press them together to hold them in position. Continue rolling with the new sheet.

**5** When you have used up all three sheets, press the final edge into the body of the candle to hold it in place. Trim the wick so that it is about ½ inch long.

When a reunion of family and friends is organized the emphasis should be on conversation, telling stories and sharing memories. To allow family members to mingle and chat with each other in an informal way, why not arrange a buffet meal on an old-fashioned side table? We used a combination of truly classic elements, such as beautiful table linen, woven basketware, and polished glass along with fresh flowers. This is the perfect opportunity to dust off heirlooms and bring them to the table where they will spark discussion.

# family reunion

A treasured old photo tied to a napkin is sure to rekindle fond family memories and become a real conversation piece.

A handsome homemade fruitcake is simply dressed with a wide white satin ribbon.

Cutlery wrapped in individual napkins is presented in a favorite basket.

A china footed dish forms the basis for this lovely floral centerpiece. Cottage garden flowers echo the feel of a past era, and will fill the room with their beautiful scent. Family photographs are carefully woven into the arrangement.

**MATERIALS**
wire card holder
footed dish
block of oasis, soaked
florist wire
moss
foliage and flowers
old family photographs

**1** Place the card holder in the dish.

# floral centerpiece

**2** Cut the wet oasis into cubes and arrange them in the dish to cover the base of the card holder. Secure the oasis together with florist wire.

**3** Generously cover the oasis with moss using wire to keep it in place.

**4** Add foliage and flowers, simply poking the stems into the moss and oasis, until no moss shows.

**5** Arrange the family photographs in the card holder so that they nestle among the flowers.

The combination of a great day out and delicious food is the recipe for a perfect picnic. Eating outdoors is always fun, so don't let cold weather dampen your enthusiasm: bundle up, pack some delicious food and drinks, and set out for a day in the open air. Thermoses of hot coffee or soup and hampers full of wholesome food are every bit as exciting as a summer picnic, and the bonus is that in winter you are likely to have a choice location all to yourselves. Whatever the weather, food always tastes better when eaten outdoors!

# winter picnic

A folding aluminum table (*right*) is lightweight and portable, making it a great choice for a picnic—use the appliquéd throw as a tablecloth, and hampers and wicker baskets as seats. A soft gray blanket decorated with appliquéd leaves is perfect for a winter picnic and looks great spread with food and neutral-color picnicware. If your table and hampers aren't too heavy, walk briskly to your picnic spot to work up a healthy appetite. If the weather is chilly it's also a good way to keep warm! Take a soccer ball or frisbee with you too—spurts of dashing around, having fun between eating and drinking, will enliven everyone's spirits and ensure a healthy glow when you return home.

The best picnics tend to be well thought out in advance. Store-bought picnic baskets can be costly, so why not improvise and fill baskets and boxes with your own essential items? Stylish picnicware, napkins, and a cruet set are vital for a civilized picnic spread. Thermoses filled with homemade soup or strong coffee will warm the spirit, and for a deliciously rustic touch try filling crusty rolls with lunch meat, then personalize them with a name card and a decorative felt leaf. Tied with string they will keep fresh and arrive safely at the table. Homemade or bought pies and fruitcakes are excellent winter picnic foods as they are fairly robust and can be cut up when you arrive.

A collection of wicker baskets and hampers is perfect to store and transport all your picnic essentials.

These stylish stacking plates and cups are lightweight and practical: they won't break if blown off the table by the wind!

A blanket adorned with felt leaves looks stunning, the single line of stitching down each leaf allowing the edges to flap in the breeze. The leaves are cut in a variety of autumnal colors and are carefully placed to look as though they are drifting down the blanket.

# appliquéd throw

**MATERIALS**
pencil
paper
scissors
pins
felt in autumnal
   colors
blanket
needle
embroidery thread

**1** Sketch some leaf shapes on paper. Choose the one you like best and photocopy it or trace around it to create enough leaf templates to cover the blanket. Cut out the shapes.

**2** Pin the paper leaves to the felt and cut around them.

**3** Arrange the felt leaves on the blanket and, once you are happy with the position, pin them in place.

**4** With a needle and embroidery thread, sew the leaves to the blanket with a line of stitches down the center of each leaf.

In the depths of winter when warm sunny days are a distant memory and the long dark evenings seem as though they are going to last forever, most of us feel like staying at home until things start to look brighter outside. Creating a sensual feast for your loved ones is a wonderful way to banish the midwinter blues and make the most of the chilly evenings. So close the door, snuggle up in warm clothes, and prepare for a cozy evening at home. Our senses are very delicate and a sensual table should subtly appeal to each of them.

# sensual feast

This fireside arrangement is designed to stimulate all the senses and awaken even the weariest of spirits, promoting feelings of well-being. A gorgeous mix of deep chocolate brown, cinnamon, and lavender are the perfect choices of colors to create a warm and inviting atmosphere. Chunky brown and cream tableware, chosen as much for its warm color as its texture, works beautifully with tactile materials such as linen and soft polished wood. Flowers, herbs, and aromatic foliage smell wonderful, while pine cones and candlelight look beautiful. Set in front of the flickering flames and nose-tingling aroma of a crackling open fire, this sensual table creates a truly uplifting atmosphere.

Chocolate-dipped spoons (*right*) are the ultimate indulgence! Simply dip the spoons in melted chocolate then leave to set. Drizzle dots of white chocolate over the spoons for a polka dot finish. Set tealights in small bowls filled with coffee beans: the beans gently heat up releasing some of their wonderful aroma. A rich chocolate torte indulges the tastebuds, and a hot toddy (*below*) not only smells good but feels deliciously comforting to cold hands. Decorate the dessert plates by sieving cocoa powder over a fork. The linen napkins are simply folded, ready to be handed out with wooden-handled cutlery to the lucky guests!

Raw linen napkins work well with wooden cutlery; a head of dried fennel seeds adds a decorative touch that smells great too.

A hot toddy served with a spicy cinnamon stick provides a warming welcome from the cold.

Aromatic foliage combined with fresh herbs and large cinnamon sticks create a focal point that not only looks great but will fill the room with delicious scent. Dried seed pods and pinecones bring added textural interest to the centerpiece.

**MATERIALS**
large shallow dish
2 large cinnamon
  sticks
2 large pinecones
a bunch of fresh
  herbs
linen ribbon
selection of dried
  seed pods and
  other dried items
  such as flower
  heads

# cinnamon centerpiece

**1** Lay the two large cinnamon sticks across the dish.

**2** Place the pinecones on either side of the cinnamon sticks. Tie small bunches of herbs together with linen ribbon and add them to the display.

**3** Fill in any gaps in the arrangement with dried seed pods and flower heads. (Replace the fresh herbs as they wilt.)

It is thanks to the Victorians that today's Christmas celebrations take the form they do. This used to be one of the few times of the year when the best pieces of tableware were brought out and used at the table. There were lots of important jobs to be done in preparation for the Christmas Eve meal: table linen and napkins had to be laundered and starched, glassware was cleaned to a sparkling finish, and cutlery was polished until it glistened. This table setting (*right*) aims to recreate the elegance of years gone by.

# the night before christmas

Christmas remains a very special time of the year for many people and a great opportunity to spend time with family and loved ones around a beautiful table. A Christmas Eve feast is the ideal occasion to decorate the dinner table in sophisticated style. In a break from the traditional color scheme of red, green, and gold, our Christmas table is decorated in a modern scheme of cool icy whites teamed with frosty silvers and clear glass, a theme inspired by icy mornings and frosty walks in the countryside. The scheme is pulled together with a simple but highly effective centerpiece: a footed glass bowl piled high with Christmas baubles and miniature lights that lends the table a magical warmth.

Attention to detail and the use of pure white, silver, and gold guarantee that dinner guests will be entranced. A freshly laundered white linen tablecloth provides a clean crisp surface onto which a generous handful of silver stars is scattered, adding extra sparkle to an enchanting setting. A plain linen napkin is given a touch of glamour with the addition of iron-on silver squares on a single corner. Chunky glass accessories, such as stylish coasters, and cool blue coffee cups ensure that the wintery theme runs right through the meal. Handwritten place labels tied to delicate baubles and laid at each setting invite guests to take their seats at this delightful table.

An elaborate beaded tassel makes an elegant and unusual napkin ring.

The shape of these candleholders echoes the silver stars that decorate the tablecloth.

A glass bowl filled with sparkling Christmas lights makes an entrancing centerpiece for this elegant table. The gold and silver baubles used here echo the frosty hues of the table, but the idea can be adapted to fit a traditional red-and-green setting.

**MATERIALS**
selection of silver
 and gold baubles
 and ornaments
footed glass bowl
set of white,
 shadeless
 Christmas lights

# bauble centerpiece

**1** Arrange a layer of baubles in the bottom of the bowl.

**2** Begin threading the lights between the baubles, carefully weaving the cord around the ornaments.

**3** Finish the arrangement with a layer of baubles, hiding as much of the electrical cord as you can.

Black and white is a combination that can't fail to give a table dramatic impact. Void of any color, emphasis is placed on shape, texture, and form. Black and white is a bold statement that would work for a lunch or dinner table, but stripped of any frills or fuss it is not for the fainthearted. For a monochromatic scheme to work, only the purest white and truest black should be used. Bone china is the perfect choice for crockery because of its whiter-than-white quality. When selecting black items be careful not to be fooled by very dark brown, green, or blue items.

# black and white

The geometric style of this table setting is achieved through use of very plain, simple shapes. The severe lines of the square bowls are complemented by the raised bumps of the platter beneath, and the snaking tealight holders contrast with the straight lines on the black and white checkered plates. Solid, robust cutlery and chunky black glass tumblers help to give the table design a very strong look, and napkins add an element of textural softness to contrast with the hard china surfaces. The spiral place mats combine black and white in concentric circles to add the final touch to this dramatic table.

Adding pattern is not something to be afraid of in a monochromatic scheme; we even included (*right*) a chinoiserie plate. Layering different-size plates and bowls creates pattern too, and looks effective when patterned pieces are interspersed with plain ones. It is possible to bring in black and white elements with food too: white rice on black china looks wonderful, as does a heap of pure white sugar cubes in a black bowl. A variety of checkered and striped napkins looks good with plain and patterned crockery. Buy a length of three or four black-and-white fabrics, cut them into squares, and hem them for perfectly coordinated table linen.

A chain of perfectly white ceramic tealight holders winds its way across the table.

One extravagant, contemporary ceramic platter is all that is needed to make a stunning design statement.

White circular place mats are decorated with a very simple concentric black circle design to create a strong design statement for the table. Materials listed to the right are for one place mat only: increase them appropriately for your chosen number.

**MATERIALS**
selection of different-size
   plates to use as
   templates
white circular place mat
   15 inches in diameter
2½ yards black hat elastic
pencil
needle
black thread
scissors

# spiral place mats

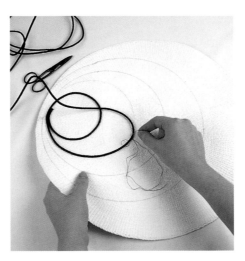

**1** Using the plates as templates mark out four concentric circles in pencil on the place mat, beginning with the largest plate and working down in size. (Begin tracing around each plate from the same point.)

**2** Lay the elastic over the pencil guidelines. Stitch the elastic to the place mat using couch stitch: starting from underneath the mat, pass the thread over the elastic and back through the mat.

**3** Continue sewing until the design is complete. Secure the end of the elastic with a few final stitches and tie off the end of the thread on the underside of the mat.

# list of projects

Italic text signifies "mini makes".
The other entries are step-by-step projects.

# acknowledgments

The author and publishers would like to thank the following organizations for lending us pieces for the book:

**Afternoon Tea** (page 24)
"Chintz" and "Old Country Roses" china courtesy of Royal Albert.
Web site: www.royal-doulton.com

**Beach Party** (page 36)
"Shore" china courtesy of Royal Doulton.
Web site: www.royal-doulton.com

**Nautical lunch** (page 46)
Sisal rope courtesy of:
W.R. Outhwaite & Son Ropemakers
Town Foot
Hawes
North Yorkshire DL8 3NT
Web site: www.ropemakers.co.uk

**Black and White** (page 112)
"Black Aves" china courtesy of Royal Crown Derby.
Web site: www.royal-crown-derby.co.uk

All craft materials were kindly supplied by:
HomeCrafts Direct
PO Box 38
Leicester
LE1 9BU
Web site: www.homecrafts.co.uk

**AUTHOR'S ACKNOWLEDGMENTS**
I would like to thank Lisa and Derek Bennett for lending us their garden for French Bistro (page 40); Vicky Lias and the Beckenham Allotment Society for a lovely morning shooting Garden Gathered (page 74), and Penny Harrison of HomeCrafts Direct for supplying all the wonderful crafts materials. Special thanks go to photographer Shona Wood, who is always lovely to work with. Last but not least, to my husband Paul for his support, patience, and good humor.

Jo Rigg

Photographed by **Shona Wood**
Designed by **Lisa Tai**
Edited by **Katy Lord**
Managed by **Janet Ravenscroft**